BRUSSELS
THE CITY AT A GLANCE

Belgacom Towers
These two mirrored high-rises, joined sky bridge, overlook the city's north q
See p014

Dexia Tower
Embedded microprocessors illumina this tower's 4,200 windows, creating of colour that light up its façade at night.
11 place Charles Rogier

Cathedral of St Michael and St Gudula
The national church of Belgium is a fine example of Brabant Gothic architecture, with intricately carved limestone towers.
Parvis Sainte Gudule

Finance Tower
This government building has been renovated and given a coat of reflective glass, in keeping with the current trend in the city.
30 boulevard du Jardin Botanique

Place du Grand Sablon
This cobbled square is lined with antiques stores and galleries, and has an eclectic array of restaurants and bars.

Astro Tower
Completed in 1976, the 107m-tall Astro Tower is easily recognised thanks to its shimmering bronze-tinted glass façade.
14 avenue de l'Astronomie

Place Royale
This square is at the heart of the museums district and backs onto the Palais Royal.

Parc de Bruxelles
Fountains, statues and tree-lined gravel paths make this park a favourite spot to escape the hustle and bustle of the city.

INTRODUCTION
THE CHANGING FACE OF THE URBAN SCENE

Brussels is resurgent. Long neglected by city powers and its transient residents, a brighter capital is emerging. And with it, renewed civic pride; not easy to achieve in such a diverse cultural environment, in which Muslim and North and West African enclaves rub shoulders with a nomadic Eurocrat population. And, of course, there is the ridiculously overblown Flemish/French language divide.

As the scaffolding has finally come down on myriad delayed renovations, the renamed Finance Tower (30 boulevard du Jardin Botanique) has appeared in shiny new clothes and the gilded dome of the Palais de Justice (see p012) now glints in the sun, as does the Atomium (see p058), polished to celebrate its 50th year in 2008. New centres for culture are re-energising the creative scene, with Flagey (see p013) leading the way. The dance centre Les Brigittines (see p060) and the contemporary arts facility Wiels (see p068) have also taken up residence in previously abandoned buildings, giving focus to some of the grittier neighbourhoods. The city is also developing a calendar of events that sees April's Art Brussels and Design September both becoming increasingly important in anchoring a raft of other festivals year round.

Food is revered here and, rather than the celebrity chef, it's what's on the plate that does the talking, while a wave of fashion talent is enhancing the city's reputation for the avant-garde. Brussels takes time to unlock but that is part of its charm, and where we come in.

ESSENTIAL INFO
FACTS, FIGURES AND USEFUL ADDRESSES

TOURIST OFFICE
Brussels Info Place
2 rue Royale
T 02 513 8940
www.brusselsinternational.be

TRANSPORT
Car hire
Budget
T 02 712 0840
Hertz
T 02 720 6044
Public transport
STIB
T 07 023 2000
stib.be
Taxis
Taxis Bleus
T 02 268 0000
www.taxisbleus.be
Taxis Verts
T 02 349 4949
www.taxisverts.be

EMERGENCY SERVICES
Ambulance/Fire
T 100
Police
T 101
24-hour pharmacy
Call for daily rota
T 07 066 0160

CONSULATES
British Consulate
85 rue d'Arlon
T 02 287 6211
ukinbelgium.fco.gov.uk/en
US Consulate
27 boulevard du Régent
T 02 508 2111
belgium.usembassy.gov

MONEY
American Express
100 boulevard du Souverain
T 02 676 2121
travel.americanexpress.com

POSTAL SERVICES
Post Office
Place de la Monnaie
02 201 2345
Shipping
DHL
671 boulevard de la Deuxième
Armée Britannique
T 02 715 5050

BOOKS
Modern Architecture in Brussels by Patrick Burniat, Pierre Puttemans and Jos Vandenbreeden (Les Editions de l'Octagon)
The Professor by Charlotte Brontë (Wordsworth Classics)
Brüsel: Cities of the Fantastic by François Schuiten and Benoît Peeters (NBM)

WEBSITES
Architecture
www.fondationpourlarchitecture.be
Newspaper
lesoir.be

COST OF LIVING
Taxi from Brussels airport to city centre
£22
Cappuccino
£2.35
Packet of cigarettes
£5.40
Daily newspaper
£1.40
Bottle of champagne
£50

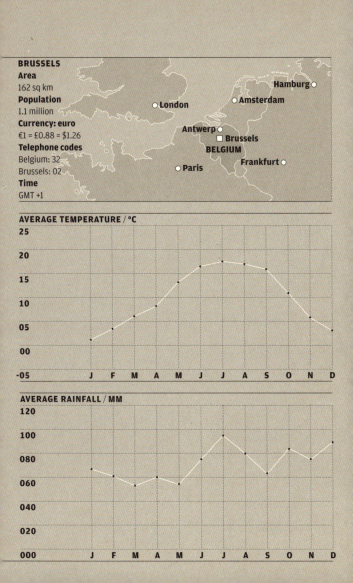

BRUSSELS
Area
162 sq km
Population
1.1 million
Currency: euro
€1 = £0.88 = $1.26
Telephone codes
Belgium: 32
Brussels: 02
Time
GMT +1

NEIGHBOURHOODS
THE AREAS YOU NEED TO KNOW AND WHY

To help you navigate the city, we've chosen the most interesting districts (see below and the map inside the back cover) and colour-coded our featured venues, according to their location; those venues that are outside these areas are not coloured.

UPPER TOWN
The ordered streets of the Upper Town were once the home of the aristocracy, and the Palais Royal overlooks Parc de Bruxelles. Many interesting museums surround Place Royale, from where you can see the magnificent dome of the Palais de Justice (see p012). Drop down the escarpment to reach the Lower Town.

ST JOSSE AND SCHAERBEEK
The glass high-rises of this north-eastern quarter, dominated by the Belgacom Towers (see p014), loom over the brooding, functionalist Gare du Nord. Closer to town is the Jardin Botanique (236 rue Royale, T 02 226 1211) and close by, appropriately enough, is Hotel Bloom (see p018).

ST GILLES AND FOREST
Forest benefits from a couple of parks that career down the slopes from the highest point in Brussels, Place de l'Altitude, with its art deco St Augustin church (see p064). Some inspired examples of art nouveau architecture, such as Hôtel Hannon (see p062), can be found in suburban St Gilles.

EU QUARTER AND ETTERBEEK
Huge areas of this neighbourhood were destroyed to make way for the institutions of the European Union, and landmark buildings such as the European Parliament (60 rue Wiertz, T 02 284 2111) and Berlaymont (see p010), home to the European Commission, now dominate.

LOWER TOWN
This was historically an area of traders and merchants, and their legacy is the gilded splendour of Grand Place. The fashion strip of rue Antoine Dansaert is where you will find Natan XIII (see p073) and Stijl (see p076). To the south is earthy Marolles, home to Bazaar (see p051), a bar, restaurant and club rolled into one.

JETTE, LAEKEN AND HEYSEL
This would be an unremarkable suburb were it not for the Tour & Taxis complex within the renovated Royal Warehouse (see p056) by the canal, the striking Atomium (see p058) and the King Baudouin Stadium (see p090), formerly Heysel, one of Belgium's largest sports grounds.

IXELLES AND UCCLE
This district is home to embassies galore and a large expat community, who frequent the lively bars and restaurants around Place du Châtelain and Place Flagey. Architectural gems include the art nouveau Horta Museum (see p067) and the art deco Museum Van Buuren (see p028).

ANDERLECHT AND MOLENBEEK
The Charleroi canal and the industrial revolution gave this area, now populated by a largely immigrant community, the nickname 'Little Manchester'. Hotels such as Be Manos (see p022) are opening up and the stretch of Anderlecht opposite rue Dansaert is showing signs of gentrification.

LANDMARKS
THE SHAPE OF THE CITY SKYLINE

Navigation in Brussels is simple given its compact centre within the *petite ceinture* (inner ring road). This pentagon-shaped route follows the city's second defensive wall, the best preserved part of which is the Porte de Hal (boulevard du Midi, T 02 534 1518). Running north-east to south-west, an escarpment splits the inner area. In Lower Town, narrow medieval lanes spread out from one of the most beautiful market squares in Europe, Grand Place, which is dominated by the baroque majesty of the guild houses. In Upper Town, wealthy Francophiles built their mansions among a more orderly street layout around the royal palace and gardens.

For an overview of the city, head for Place Poelaert in front of the imposing Palais de Justice (see p012), from where the Basilique du Sacré-Cœur de Koekelberg (1 parvis de la Basilique, T 02 425 8822) and the sparkle of the Atomium (see p058) are clear. Take a glance along rue de la Régence to get an idea of the grand boulevards King Leopold II was working towards in one of the few concentrated eras of town planning the city has seen.

Head down rue de la Loi to discover the Berlaymont (overleaf), the building that dominates the EU Quarter, and the triumphal arch of Palais du Cinquantenaire. Avenue Louise leads to the Ixelles ponds and Flagey (see p013) in Place Sainte-Croix, and chaussée d'Alsemberg heads up to St Augustin Church (see p064).
For full addresses, see Resources.

Berlaymont
Designed by Lucien de Vestel, the hulking HQ of the European Commission opened in 1967, its cruciform shape dominating the Schuman roundabout. A full-scale renovation, which was completed in 2004, upped its eco credentials, and the façade is now covered with glass louvres, which move automatically to regulate temperature and reduce glare.
200 rue de la Loi

Palais de Justice

Joseph Poelart

Like most of the neoclassical buildings in the city, the Palais de Justice was commissioned by King Leopold II, who insisted that its proportions be greater than St Peter's Basilica in Rome (they are). Designed by the architect Joseph Poelaert, the building was one of the largest in the world when it was completed in 1883, and at 26,000 sq m it is still preposterous. Even harder to comprehend than its scale is the mishmash of neoclassical styles and the architectural faux pas that has huge columns blocking light from the windows. It remains a functioning court and lawyers in ermine-lined stoles can be seen whispering with clients in dark corners. The king's megalomaniacal vision is worth a visit, but the building fails to deliver the knockout blow he would have expected.
Place Poelaert, T 02 508 6410

Joseph Diongre

Flagey
Nicknamed the *Paquebot Jaune* (Yellow Steamer), this imperious building was formerly the National Institute for Radio Broadcasting. Designed by Joseph Diongre in the 1930s, its art deco detailing was restored in 2002. Now a cultural centre known simply as Flagey, it includes several auditoriums with exceptional acoustics. The building presides over Place Eugène Flagey, which was a nightmarish traffic junction before German-based urban landscape specialists Latz + Partner pedestrianised it. Now it's a welcoming space with sweeping benches that sit under reintroduced greenery. Thanks to a moment of joined-up thinking, even the glass roof of the tram and bus shelter sits on tree-trunk-like steel supports.
Place Sainte-Croix, T 02 641 1020, www.flagey.be

Belgacom Towers
These two 28-storey towers are the HQ of the Belgian telephone company. In 1996 the existing structure was given a facelift by M & J-M Jaspers – J Eyers & Partners, who added the mirrored façade and an air-bridge linking the perpendicularly aligned buildings. With a little bit of imagination, the reflection of the clouds on the towers blends them with the sky.
Koning Albert II-laan

HOTELS

WHERE TO STAY AND WHICH ROOMS TO BOOK

The capital's new-found appetite for creativity is well catered for by a plethora of new boutique hotels, many of which are featured here, together with the classiest five-star in town, the Hotel Amigo (see p020). Nearby is the Royal Windsor Hotel (5 rue Duquesnoy, T 02 505 5555), where the Fashion Rooms – corner suites decorated by Belgian fashion talents such as Jean-Paul Knott and Kaat Tilley – are the antithesis of the gilt-laden fussiness of the public areas. Just to the north is the grande dame in town, the 1895 Hotel Metropole (31 place de Brouckère, T 02 217 2300), whose opulent lobby recalls the city's fin-de-siècle heyday. There are numerous branded hotels but not many new ones: the first Aloft hotel (place Jean Rey, T 02 224 3199) in Europe is due to open in late 2010; the Sofitel Brussels Le Louise (40 avenue de la Toison d'Or, T 02 514 2200), refurbished in 2008, is well positioned for the shopping on avenue Louise; while the Crowne Plaza Brussels City Centre – Le Palace (3 rue Gineste, T 02 203 6200) on Place Rogier has an art nouveau feel. The dominance of business travellers can make for expensive midweek stays but discounts at weekends.

For a more intimate experience, choose from the four beautiful rooms designed by Philippe Guilmin at Chambres en Ville (19 rue de Londres, T 02 512 9290) or the three austere but stylish rooms at Hooy Kaye Lodge (22 quai aux Pierres de Taille, T 02 218 4440). *For full addresses and room rates, see Resources.*

Hotel Café Pacific
By night, a wash of blue lights up the ornate façade of this 12-room hotel in the heart of the Flemish quarter. The original 1930 art nouveau wood panelling and brass fittings of the street-level café were retained during the reconstruction of the building, and architect Marc Humblet cleverly integrated a lift into the narrow floorplan. Opened as a hotel in 2007, the rooms have been given a modern look with oak floorboards, opaque glass and white leather upholstery accented with splashes of maroon in the soft furnishings, which are supplied by Mia Zia of Morocco. Our favourite is Mezzanine Room 201 (above), with its freestanding bath and strips of paper with Edith Piaf song lyrics hanging from pink wind chimes above the bed.
57 rue Antoine Dansaert, T 02 213 0080, hotelcafepacific.com

Hotel Bloom
This is not an art hotel and yet each of its 305 rooms is decorated with a unique fresco around the headboard. A slim horizontal mirror on the opposite wall allows contemplation of the work from the bed. Students at leading European art colleges and universities were asked to interpret the word 'bloom', and this has delivered a kaleidoscopic array of designs, from the minimal red circles of Scot Brian Dickson's Heartbeat Room 209 to the cartoon frenzy of Fin Timo Vaittinen in Room 331. We prefer something a little more comforting to sleep beneath, such as the petal motifs by Korean Soo Kyung Kwon in Room 326 (above).
250 rue Royale, T 02 220 6611,
www.hotelbloom.com

HOTELS

Hotel Amigo
The elegant mix of contemporary and vintage furniture here is typical of the interiors of Rocco Forte hotels. Inspired by the antiques stores just up the slope around Place du Grand Sablon, the Presidential Suite René Magritte (above) is especially influenced by pieces sold by the dealer Michel Lambrecht (T 02 502 2729). It is our room of choice given its colourful style, even if it missed a trick celebrating the surrealist after whom it is named. Other guest rooms incorporate Magritte prints and amusing sculptural references to Hergé's *Tintin* characters, which decorate the spacious bathrooms. Over-stitched hessian wall hangings from the Belgian Congo bring the country's history into the hotel interiors.
1-3 rue de l'Amigo, T 02 547 4747, hotelamigo.com

The White Hotel
Curated by Lise Coirier, founder of creative consultancy Pro Materia, this hotel is essentially a large vitrine showcasing contemporary Belgian design talent. The 53 rooms of this former apartment block all feature furniture by local designers alongside an Eames classic or two. Most of the pieces, such as the steel 'PicNik' table by Xavier Lust and Dirk Wynants or the '03' chair and 'MVS' chaise by Maarten Van Severen for Vitra, are available to buy. The monochrome colour scheme of the large guest rooms, such as the Super White (above) is stylishly done. A 55m wave-like laminated wood counter links the front desk to the bar, with its 'M2' series of modular foam furniture by Scott Wilson for Belgian design company Quinze & Milan.
212 avenue Louise, T 02 644 2929, thewhitehotel.be

Be Manos
Lighting up the gritty rag-trade area around the Thalys & Eurostar terminus are the chic interiors of the Be Manos hotel. This blast from the 1960s has splashes of crimson, lime and orange reminiscent of Mary Quant's colour tones. Tinkling in the lobby bar (above) are veils of sequined chainmail by Le Labo Design. Smoky bronze and chrome add to the masculine, urbane style that is continued in the 30 sq m rooms, where a mix of slate, leather, Plexiglas, wood and stainless steel will send your haptic sense into overdrive. Ask for either of the two rear-facing Junior Suites with terraces overlooking the courtyard. The light and airy Be Lella restaurant serves a great selection of beautifully prepared Belgian staples.
23 square de l'Aviation, T 02 520 6565, bemanos.com

The Dominican

Located on the site of a 15th-century abbey, there's nothing ascetic about the Dominican. Opened as a hotel in 2007, the cloistered courtyard of vaulted arcades has been recreated, and a Gothic-inspired pattern taken from the friars' vestments is used as a decorative element in the carpets and light screens. Otherwise it is all indulgent luxury from Amsterdam-based design duo FG Stijl. Twin fireplaces set the tone in the entrance and the Grand Lounge is furnished with pieces upholstered in rich velvets and suedes from its 'AngloDutch' range for Interna. Guest rooms are done out in neutral, coral red, petrol blue or deep green; we suggest the Twin Deluxe Room 531 (above) or one of the Junior Suites with additional lounge area.
9 rue Leopold, T 02 203 0808, thedominican.be

24 HOURS
SEE THE BEST OF THE CITY IN JUST ONE DAY

The polished neighbourhoods of Ixelles and Uccle are cherished by their expat and local communities and less trampled by the tourist hordes than Upper and Lower Town. Our itinerary takes you on a stroll through these broad, tree-lined boulevards to the south of the city. The Museum & Gardens Van Buuren (see p028), the house of a financier whose art collection was bequeathed to the public, is an art deco triumph, but keep your eyes peeled for the architectural treats round every corner. *Sgraffito* (scratched plaster) frescoes compete with faux-Gothic turrets, cobblestoned streets and art deco tiling – just watch out for dog mess, the scourge of a city of flat-dwellers with a penchant for designer pooches.

After breakfast at Gaudron (opposite), browse the interiors boutiques around Place Georges Brugmann, such as Faisons un Rêve (see p077), Scènes de Ménage (4 place Georges Brugmann, T 02 344 3295) and Alexis Vanhove (61 rue Émile Bouilliot). After the serenity of the Xavier Hufkens gallery (overleaf), make your way to the Ixelles ponds, taking in streets such as rue Vilain XIV and rue de la Vallée, where Victor Horta, Ernest Blerot and the Delune brothers have left a rich art nouveau heritage. The urbane interior of Kif Kif Café (see p030) provides a welcome stop for tea and cake. Jump in a taxi and head into town for dinner at Comme Chez Soi (see p031), the city's most celebrated restaurant.
For full addresses, see Resources.

10.00 Gaudron

This deli/pâtisserie/restaurant's elegant white interior, designed by Barbara Ferret, is brought to life by a colourful array of carefully displayed products, such as Clément Faugier tinned chestnuts and bottles of organic lemonade. Arrive early at weekends to get a table on the south-facing pavement terrace to sample owner/chef Pierre Mendrowski's brunch menu. Savouries such as eggs Benedict or *assiette gaudron à fond la forme*, including grilled vegetables, quinoa, tabouleh and smoked salmon, are served along with delicious pastries. Even the toilets are a visual treat thanks to the cartoon artwork by Denis Meyers.
3 place Georges Brugmann,
T 02 343 9790, gaudron.be

12.00 Xavier Hufkens

Belgian architects Robbrecht en Daem and Marie-José Van Hee have created a wonderfully open gallery space, with grey poured concrete floors and whitewashed pillars, overlooking neatly manicured gardens. Past exhibitions have included works on paper by Willem de Kooning and Louise Bourgeois, sculpture by Ken Price and Antony Gormley, and installations by Roni Horn, including her *Untitled (Isabelle Huppert)* photo series and *Opposite of White v1* sculpture (both right). The Brussels art scene is gaining in strength every year, so it is no surprise that the city has witnessed the arrival of galleries from New York dealer Barbara Gladstone (T 02 513 3531) and Almine Rech from Paris (T 02 648 5684).
6-8 rue Saint-Georges, T 02 639 6730, xavierhufkens.com

14.00 Museum Van Buuren

The Van Buuren family left their steeply gabled home and its cornucopia of art to the public in 1973. The interiors are a snapshot of art deco styles and include a bronze and coloured glass chandelier by Jan Eisenloeffel and carpets by J Gidding as well as art by Gustave Van de Woestijne and Constant Permeke.
41 avenue Leo Errera, T 02 343 4851. museumvanbuuren.com

17.00 Kif Kif Café
It's hard to beat Kif Kif's refreshing mint tea and heavenly, honeyed pastries, delivered daily by Algerian pâtisserie La Bague de Kenza in Paris. The lounge area (above) of this unpretentious eaterie abuts the restaurant where the Israeli- and Mediterranean-influenced menu includes an extensive mezze served as 'mini-kifs' of tahini, hummus and falafel. Formerly a petrol station, Kif Kif's interior was transformed by graphic-design duo Eric Weise and François van den Bergen of Troisbarrespoint. The design concept centres on the adventures of a fictitious Algerian astronaut, whose postcards and medals decorate the walls, along with bespoke and retro light fittings and mirrored wallpaper cutouts. In summer, a terrace offers views of the Ixelles ponds.
1 square Biarritz, T 02 644 1810

20.00 Comme Chez Soi
This family-run gourmet restaurant holds the maximum 19 points from Gault Millau and two Michelin stars. Amid acres of starched white linen, dinner here is memorable, from the delicious *amuse-gueules* to the divine petits fours. It's worth building up an appetite for dishes such as sautéed scallops with Parmesan ice cream, Belgian chicory stuffed with jugged hare, and steamed John Dory with shiitake bouillon and Chinese chive. If the amber warmth of the dining room's art nouveau interior looks too good to be true, that is because it is a faithful reproduction completed in 1988 by interior design firm Simonis. There's also a 25,000-bottle wine cellar, including a good selection of Pétrus.
23 place Rouppe, T 02 512 2921, www.commechezsoi.be

URBAN LIFE
CAFÉS, RESTAURANTS, BARS AND NIGHTCLUBS

They take their dining seriously in this culinary capital. From the two-Michelin-starred Comme Chez Soi (see p031) to pizza by the kilo at Mamma Roma (5 rue du Page, T 02 544 1402), there is high-quality and well-priced food to be found. For seafood, head to the old fish market on Place Sainte-Catherine, where street stalls compete with the unpretentious La Boussole (61 quai au Bois à Brûler, T 02 218 5877) and Bij den Boer (60 quai aux Briques, T 02 512 6122). For haute cuisine, try the Sea Grill (Radisson SAS Royal Hotel, 47 rue de Fossé aux Loups, T 02 227 9225) or the oyster bar at Belga Queen (32 rue du Fossé aux Loups, T 02 217 2187).

Lower Town is packed with good restaurants and bars, but avoid the hawking waiters around Grand Place. You will also be spoilt for choice in Ixelles and Uccle, particularly between Place Brugmann and Place du Châtelain. Top-notch cuisine pulls in locals at En Face de Parachute (578 chaussée de Waterloo, T 02 346 4741), La Quincaillerie (45 rue du Page, T 02 533 9833) and Portrait de Famille (165a rue Franz Merjay, T 02 344 3712).

The city's bar scene is eclectic and terraces tend to get packed when the sun's out. Belgium is home to InBev, the world's largest brewer, but many micro-operations are also going strong; Chez Moeder Lambic (see p039) leads the way. The club scene (see p051) can be fickle; consult Noctis (noctis.com) for the latest happenings. *For full addresses, see Resources.*

Le Canne en Ville

For the best steak in town look no further than the kitchen of chef Christian Schmit. The Irish beef, from butchers Jack O'Shea's (T 02 732 5351), will be cooked *bleu*, *saignant* or *à point*, so don't ask for 'well done' — you will be advised to choose something else. The Belgian/French menu includes dishes such as scampi with tapenade and aubergine caviar, grey shrimp and Riesling mash, duck, beef carpaccio, chateaubriand and foie gras. The large windows, Paris Métro wall tiles and steel hooks give the game away for this former butchery, a restaurant for more than 25 years. This is a gentlemanly place with the bonhomie of a family-run business that takes extreme pride in what it does.
22 rue de la Réforme, T 02 347 2926, www.lacanneenville.be

Café Walvis
Flemish for whale, this canalside bar/eaterie boasts a metallic interior by Fred Nicolay, in keeping with the edginess of the area, with black-painted corrugated iron lining the walls and shelving of wires and steel tubes. During the day the terrace is a popular choice, and in the evening a DJ attracts a lively crowd.
209 rue Antoine Dansaert,
T 02 219 9532, cafewalvis.be

Lola

The pared-down interior and varied menu at Lola are popular with well-heeled fashionistas. It's perfect for a lazy Sunday afternoon lunch following a scout around the Grand Sablon antiques stores and art galleries, and gets extremely busy, so you'll need to book. For similar quality food in a more vibrant, arty venue, try Au Vieux Saint Martin (T 02 512 6476) – its terrace is well positioned for people-watching.

Alternatively, the neighbourly *estaminet* Chez Richard (T 02 512 1406) is good for a plate of freshly shucked oysters or *stoemp*, a local delicacy of creamed mashed potato, with the added variables of root vegetables, bacon, herbs and spices.
33 place du Grand Sablon, T 02 514 2460, restolola.be

L'Artea
Behind a tall laurel hedge next to the Bois de la Cambre, Brussels' take on Central Park, hides this little gem. The terrace is the real draw, but given the fickle Belgian weather, the restaurant's conservatory is a good alternative. The fresh, taupe-coloured décor is understated and lets the food do the talking. The menu is influenced by owner José Tarea's Italian heritage and includes classics such as osso bucco and saltimbocca, well supported by a French-heavy wine list. The house dessert *dame blanche* (whipped cream and hot chocolate sauce over vanilla ice cream) is a must.
940 chaussée de Waterloo, T 02 372 0979

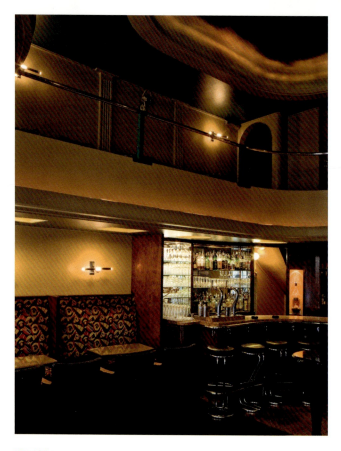

L'Archiduc
The foggy leaded lights in the windows and the bouncer on the door add to the mystique of this small, happening bar. It is always packed with a non-conformist crowd – think tattoos, beanies and foppish-haired arty types. There is live early-evening jazz on Saturdays and Sundays centred around the piano, and a wide range of cocktails is somehow served from the unfeasibly tiny bar. The original art deco interior is bathed in low, green-gold light, which is reflected by two chrome-clad columns. If you want a bit of privacy, head upstairs to the narrow mezzanine, which is perfect for checking out the crowd below.
6 rue Antoine Dansaert, T 02 512 0652, archiduc.net

Chez Moeder Lambic

They take their beer seriously at Chez Moeder Lambic, but there are plenty of comic moments. While you might not get to see barman Jean Philippe's Hawaiian-print shirts on every visit, you can always raise a smile by ordering a Saison Silly or, at a punchy 7.5 per cent alcohol, a Sloeber from Oudenaarde. The dusty bottles displayed in the windows and heavy wooden tables are part of the charm of this place; but note the sparkle of the glasses above the handpumps. None of the 200-plus beers are from mainstream suppliers, so you will need some advice from the staff, all of whom are passionate about the brown stuff. To learn more, join a tasting session in the cellar (overleaf), which is crammed with Lambic beers, brewed using traditional techniques.
68 rue de Savoie, T 02 544 1699

Cellar, Chez Moeder Lambic

URBAN LIFE

Brasseries Georges

Don't be deterred by the brash red neon strip lights on the exterior of Brasseries Georges. Instead, look beyond the wide terrace to the bank of crustacea, molluscs and other seafood on ice, and the grandiose fin-de-siècle-style interiors (mosaic floors, brass fittings and stained-glass windows). The cod with olive-oil mash is excellent, as are the unusual cuts of beef served with frites cooked in your choice of beef or goose fat, or olive oil. Service is efficient if occasionally brusque, and it's all professionally done, making Brasseries Georges a reliable choice for a casual or more formal lunch or dinner. In a similar, traditional vein are the more centrally located Roue d'Or (T 02 514 2554) and Restaurant Vincent (T 02 511 2607), with its glazed-tile seascape panoramas.
*259 avenue Winston Churchill,
T 02 347 2100, brasseriesgeorges.be*

Bar du Matin
There is more to this workaday bar near Place Albert than meets the eye. Notable design aspects include the wide glass frontage that overlooks the pavement terrace and the swirling contours of the ceiling, which was the creation of architects AAC and local bar-design guru Fred Nicolay. Pick up an international paper from the bar to go with your freshly pressed orange juice or cuppa – the *thé de Bruxelles* is an aromatic combination of nougat, hazelnut and *spéculoos*, a local ginger biscuit. If you need something more substantial, the small chiller cabinet holds a limited selection of sandwiches and salads. The no-smoking policy disappears at night when regular DJ sessions draw an eclectic crowd from the local neighbourhood.
172 chaussée d'Alsemberg, T 02 537 7159

Café des Spores

The deep colours of the painted stripes on the walls and ceilings give this popular, cosy local an unexpected air of sophistication. As the name suggests, it's all about mushrooms here. The blackboard menu changes daily, but there are normally a couple of excellent standards. The crumble of snowball mushrooms with roasted almonds, olives and grilled tomatoes is a sublime appetiser. Follow this with the shiitake stuffed with pork and veal, and you may just have room for the sweet-and-savoury crème brûlée made with cèpes and foie gras. Wash it all down with a powerful red from the largely organic wine cellar.
103-108 chaussée d'Alsemberg,
T 02 534 1303, cafedesspores.be

Le Balmoral

When you spot the baby-pink Volkswagen Beetle or the powder-blue Auto Union scooter outside, you know you've arrived at the city's only American-style diner. This is mostly a brunch venue, popular at weekends. The 1950s-influenced interior is a mix of rounded forms, pastel colours and chrome fittings. Murals by local artist Stéphane Dubray, such as *James Dean in Brussels*, sit above vinyl banquettes. The Megaburger has all the trimmings, and shakes are well represented on a menu that leans towards Tex Mex. Other good eateries nearby include the Winery (T 02 345 4717) and lunchtime-only restaurant L'Intemporelle (T 02 345 9893).
*21 place Georges Brugmann,
T 02 347 0882, sites.resto.com/balmoral*

Taverne Greenwich
Rarely busy, this traditional bolt-hole is like walking into a time warp. Nothing seems to have changed since Magritte used to try to flog his pictures here. Even some of the old boys clacking away with the chess and draughts pieces seem to have been here forever, joined today by creatives tapping away at their Macs while enjoying a leisurely beer; you'd be hard-pressed to find a more authentic bar in Brussels. For a little more life, try the next-door bar/restaurant Fin de Siècle (9 rue des Chartreux) or head to the strip of rue du Marché au Charbon, where local staple Fontainas (T 02 503 3112) is to be found.
7 rue des Chartreux, T 02 511 4167

Bonsoir Clara

The court-jester colours of the Mondrian-esque wall coverings are the defining feature of this restaurant. Inspired by a vibrant shop window display by Agnès Emery (see p085), designer Fred Nicolay had the material run up by a local seamstress and then reproduced it in back-lit glass on the opposite wall (above). The menu includes roast lamb with a wasabi crust and tangerine and date sauce, and lemon-marinated chicken with green curry and basmati rice, as well as Belgian staples such as *croquettes crevettes grises* (sweet grey shrimps).
22-26 rue Antoine Dansaert,
T 02 502 0990, bonsoirclara.be

La Manufacture
Located on the site of a former leather factory, which supplied luxury-goods firm Delvaux, this aptly named restaurant continues the industrial theme with block-end wooden flooring, steel columns and exposed ducts. Red granite-topped tables sit beneath rough-plastered walls painted blood-red. The bamboo in the courtyard goes some way to softening the austere red-brick and grey-concrete exterior. The hearty Belgian fare includes pork knuckle, terrine of hare with pistachio, and wood pigeon with foie gras mousse. The international clientele are served by an able team led by maître d' of 15 years, Bruno, who is clearly the boss in his leather apron.
12-20 rue Notre-Dame du Sommeil, T 02 502 2525, manufacture.be

Bazaar

The richly coloured arabesque interior, glass chandeliers and mismatched furniture of this large restaurant/bar sit above the earthy brick arches of the basement club (above). Bazaar does a good trade as a one-stop venue for a lively night out and the upstairs bar is a good alternative space when the dancefloor gets too packed. Other going-out options close by include the granddaddy of the Brussels club scene and alleged birthplace of European techno, Fuse (T 02 511 9789), and the eclectic bar/restaurant Recyclart (T 02 289 0059) underneath Chapelle station. The Dirty Dancing evenings by resident DJ Cosy Mozzy at the former cinema, Mirano Continental (T 02 227 3942), are also worth a crack.
63 rue de Capucins, T 02 511 2600, bazaarresto.be

Cospaia
Designed by Marcel Wolterinck, this chic eaterie has two rooms: the first is moody and modern with black walls and wire trees; the other is white with stucco ceilings, fireplaces and parquet floors, with a gold banquette (pictured) by the bar. Service is variable, but the modern European cuisine is consistently good.
1 rue Capitaine Crespel, T 02 513 0303, cospaia.be

URBAN LIFE

INSIDER'S GUIDE
CÉLINE PÉCHEUX, CONSULTANT EDITOR

Brussels-born Céline Pécheux works on lifestyle and design titles for the publishing house Edition Ventures. She loves Sundays in the city when she'll start with brunch at Gaudron (see p025), where 'the spirit of the old bakery is still alive in the new modern setting'. In the afternoon, she'll rummage around the markets of Marolles before heading to La Cantine de la Ville (72 rue Haute, T 02 512 8898), for its 'traditional food and friendly ambience'.

Pécheux's favourite fashion shops include Privé Joke (76-78 rue Marché au Charbon, T 02 502 6367), which has a 'beautiful interior and a wide selection of brands, including a number of Brussels exclusives', and vintage store Modes (164 rue Blaes, T 02 512 4907). For a night out with friends, she is a fan of Bazaar (see p051) or the Japanese restaurant Kamo (123 avenue des Saisons, T 02 648 7848), which is named after its chef. 'I love the design there. It's also great fun trying out dishes I've never heard of before.'

Sun-dappled evenings are spent on the terrace at Le Tavernier (445 chaussée de Boondael, T 02 640 7191) or on the whitewashed decking of La Terrasse de l'Hippodrome (51-53 chaussée de la Hulpe, T 02 354 7200). On summer weekends, she joins the exodus to the beach at Knokke-Heist, where the Riverwoods Channel Club (832b Zeedijk-Het Zoute, T 05 062 8404) and, at night, Knokke Out (7 Astridlaan, T 05 060 1226) are her haunts.

For full addresses, see Resources.

ARCHITOUR
A GUIDE TO THE CITY'S ICONIC BUILDINGS

The architecture of Brussels is one of fractured dreams. The disappearance of the River Senne under grandiose boulevards; the neighbourhoods destroyed to make way for the neoclassical hulks of Leopold II and the European Commission buildings; and the north-south rail link that rudely cuts through the centre of the city all distort the urban landscape, yet provide some of its most striking features. There is an overwhelming mix of architectural styles here that sees the delicate art nouveau of Hôtel Hannon (see p062) and the Horta Museum (see p067) jostling with the pared-down art deco of St Augustin Church (see p064) and the sleek modernism of the Glaverbel building (see p070). A disregard for planning and rampant property speculation from the 1970s to the 1990s has meant that countless bland residential blocks, ridiculous in their lack of compatibility, tower over Brussels' Gothic gems.

The upside of the realisation that the city's image was being undermined has led to an increase in the scope of revitalisation. The clean-up of the area around Grand Place and the redevelopment of the 1900 Royal Warehouse into the Tour & Taxis complex (86c avenue du Port, T 02 420 6069), with shops, offices and restaurants, are two of several initiatives signalling the boost in regeneration. There might not be vast amounts of new builds, but Brussels' existing architecture is gradually being given a new lease of life.
For full addresses, see Resources.

CBR Administrative Offices
The uniform pattern and curvaceous mouth-like openings of Marcel Lambrich's office building, which was completed in 1970, create a harmonious composition. The bronze-glass-mirrored windows reflect the suburban location and leave the façade uncluttered by the detritus of office life inside. At night, lighting accentuates the form of the prefabricated panels that are a celebration of the products made by CBR, the cement company that is headquartered here. The lobby is home to sculptures in white cement, such as *Silhouette* by Maria Kasimir. The adjacent Generali Real Estate Investments block (187-189 chaussée de la Hulpe) tries to pull off a similar look with tinted windows, but its grubbiness only serves to highlight its neighbour's beauty.
185 chaussée de la Hulpe

Atomium

The centrepiece of Expo 58, André Waterkeyn's design was based on an iron molecule magnified 165 billion times, with each globe representing an atom. In 2004, a renovation project began and lighting by Ingo Maurer has since been added. There are great views from the escalators along the linking tubes.
Square de l'Atomium, boulevard du Centenaire, T 02 475 4747, atomium.be

Les Brigittines
The contours, footprint and volume of architect Andrea Bruno's Cor-ten steel-and-glass structure mimic those of the 17th-century Les Brigittines chapel, both used as performance spaces for the Contemporary Arts Centre for Movement and Voice. The collaboration between Bruno and SumProject was completed in the summer of 2007 and is one of the city's few contemporary buildings of note. The interiors incorporate state-of-the-art theatres and rehearsal studios, which are soundproofed against the railway and the gritty street life of this ravaged area of the Marolles. Quite what the hard-working folk who occupy the particularly unpleasant graffiti-spattered concrete block behind make of the prancing dancers is another matter altogether.
1 petite rue des Brigittines, T 02 213 8610, www.brigittines.be

ARCHITOUR

Hôtel Hannon
Completed in 1904, this was the only art nouveau building architect Jules Brunfaut designed. He chose a more rational and restrained approach than the baroque exuberance of his peers. Nevertheless, the sheer theatre of the entrance hall, with its swirling, tessellated mosaic floor, will take your breath away. On a summer's day, the light streaming in through the stained-glass bay window of the winter garden's loggia lights up the lakeside fresco beside the staircase. Brunfaut's beautifully sculpted, lengthy façade of Euville stone makes the most of its corner plot. The building is now home to the photographic gallery Contretype.
1 avenue de la Jonction, T 02 538 4220, contretype.org

St Augustin Church
A slow walk up towards St Augustin Church, which is located at the highest point in Brussels, reveals a stubby, geometrically patterned tower on top of a heavyweight base. Léon Guianotte and André Watteyne's structure, finished in 1935, might not have the gravitas of another of the city's art deco churches, the behemoth of the Basilique du Sacré-Coeur de Koekleberg (T 02 425 8822), but few buildings do. The simplicity of St Augustin's exterior, greatly in need of a lick of paint, is certainly not over-indulgent, and serves to focus attention on the topmost cross. The floorplan of the church follows the form of a Greek cross, with short aisles of equal length, while the sober interior is relieved by the abstract patterns in the stained-glass windows.
Place de l'Altitude Cent, T 02 344 5956

VUB Rectorate

The narrow elliptic shape of the 1976 Rectorate building at Vrije Universiteit Brussel (VUB) typifies Antwerp architect Renaat Braem's later 'biomorphic' approach. The slim, pale bricks of the façade and narrow slot windows hide a playful interior. The sweeping upturned fan of the concrete portal continues as a structural element within the small lobby, which is decorated with a red-brick frieze and blue-and-white glazed floor tiles that trace the edge of cloverleaf pillars. Throughout, the curvaceous internal walls are decorated with colourful murals that appealed to Braem's utopian ideals. Connecting the floors is a spiral staircase, a basic construction of open wooden treads and blue-lacquered metal frame that captures a pleasant simplicity of form.
2 boulevard de la Plaine

Horta Museum

The former home and studio of architect Victor Horta is an incredible ensemble of art nouveau. Built in the late 1890s, everything in the house was custom-made except for the Twyford bathroom appliances and William Morris wallpaper, both imported from Britain. To open up the narrow structure, Horta introduced a lightwell above the central staircase, which serves to illuminate its graciously curved wrought-iron balustrade. Glass, wood and mosaic are worked into the floral, arabesque and feminine silhouettes that epitomise the style. Horta was able to reinvent himself with the arrival of the art deco era, as seen in his work at the Central Station (2 carrefour de l'Europe), which is testimony to his creative genius.
25 rue Américaine, T 02 543 0490, www.hortamuseum.be

Wiels

The pillars of *pierre bleue* stone at street level give way to the vast concrete planes of the refurbished former brewery of Wielemans-Ceuppens. Commissioned in 1930, it is now used as a contemporary arts centre, but its interior is still dominated by the three remaining brass brewing kettles that poke out of the green-tiled floor. This hulking modernist structure, designed by Adrien Blomme, stands in a dubious area of town which is undergoing redevelopment, although the views over the railway tracks racing into Midi station are far from glamorous. In 2008, one of the adjacent former brewery buildings known as Brass was also converted into an entertainment space, Salle de Machines (T 02 343 2004), complete with original generators and a beautiful split-level restaurant/bookshop.
354 avenue Van Volxem,
T 02 340 0050, wiels.org

Glaverbel
Architect Renaat Braem's circular building, completed in 1967, is named after the Belgian glass manufacturer for which it was designed, and accordingly the façade is covered in a curtain of tinted windows. Inside, the circular corridors provide a view of the landscaped inner 'courtyard', but the echo of heels on the *pierre bleue* flagstones doesn't half travel.
166 chaussée de la Hulpe

SHOPPING
THE BEST RETAIL THERAPY AND WHAT TO BUY

The city's best shopping enclaves are found within Lower Town. The arcades of galerie du Roi provide opportunities for browsing fashion at Kaat Tilley (No 6, T 02 510 0012) or leafing through an art book at Librairie Saint-Hubert (see p078). Stroll along rue Antoine Dansaert and the lanes that lead off it for avant-garde retail. This stretch is home to the city's best fashion boutiques, including Stijl (see p076), Martin Margiela (see p081) and Christophe Coppens (23 place du Nouveau Marché aux Grains, T 02 538 0813), plus specialist stores such as Natan XIII (opposite) and Underwear (47 rue Antoine Dansaert, T 02 514 2731). The further towards the canal you go, the edgier it gets, with the gallery Alice (182 rue Antoine Dansaert, T 02 513 3307) and sneaker store Waffles (overleaf) breaking lots of rules.

The gentrified streets around Upper Town's Place du Grand Sablon are lined with commercial art galleries. Nearby Emery & Cie (see p085) leads the way in interiors while earthy rue Haute and rue Blaes are home to a host of antiques and interiors shops, including Jacques Brol (202 rue Haute, T 0476 250 253) and Stef's Antique Hall (63 rue Blaes). For more interesting furniture stores and boutiques, head to the area around Place George Brugmann, where you will find Faisons un Rêve (see p077) and the stationer Le Typographe (167 rue Franz Merjay, T 02 345 1676).

For full addresses, see Resources.

Natan XIII

The large corner window of rue Antoine Dansaert's most upscale accessories boutique was originally the entrance to a 1930s garage. Owner Thierry Struvay has designed an elegant shelving arrangement on which is displayed jewellery by Marie-Hélène de Taillac, bags from ex-Hermès artisan Isaac Rene and cashmere scarves by Faliero Sarti. We were drawn to the colourful beads of the 'Tamawa' collection by Atelier Verstraeten, inspired by billiard balls and made from Bakelite. There is also a 'scent cabin' where you can sample Frédéric Malle's perfumes. Ladders, replicas of those used for costume storage at the Comédie-Française theatre, stand on the original mosaic floor. The store is a collaboration with the fashion boutique Natan (T 02 647 1001).
101 rue Antoine Dansaert, T 02 514 1517

Waffles

In a city that is synonymous with *gaufres*, Dutch copywriter Ad Luijten has created a tribute to the waffle sole. Rainbow-hued trainers, many of them vintage, are displayed in foam, mirror-backed waffle-shaped wall units in an austere, all-white interior. The sales counter is a pastiche of kerbside waffle stands. *189 rue Antoine Dansaert, T 02 219 0575, ilovewaffles.be*

Stijl

Sonja Noël is the fashion forerunner who arguably began the gentrification of rue Antoine Dansaert, when she opened multi-brand store Stijl (Flemish for style) some 25 years ago. An early promoter of Belgian designers, she has literally grown up with the Antwerp Six. The steel racks let the clothes of Dries Van Noten and Ann Demeulemeester speak for themselves. Younger Belgian designers, such as Cathy Pill and Tim Van Steenbergen, are also sold here. Quality vintage clothing is available next door at Idiz Bogam (T 02 512 1032), while more upcoming talent can be seen in Aurore Jean's curvaceous creations at Mademoiselle Jean (T 02 513 5069).
74 rue Antoine Dansaert, T 02 512 0313

Faisons un Rêve

Each month the gallery-like furniture installation at Faisons un Rêve is renewed by its inspirational owner, Raymond Debessel. From his extensive stock come original midcentury pieces, including rugs and lighting, together with beautifully arranged jewellery. Look out for a strong selection of Scandinavian furniture from Hans Olsen and Johannes Andersson, plus lighting by Italians Vico Magistretti and Umberto Riva. Jewellery by Vivianna Torun and Hans Hansen sits alongside a collection of vibrant pieces designed by the Mexican modernist Antonio Pineda. The store's name translates as 'let's make a dream' and Debessel certainly helps his clients fulfil theirs.

112 avenue Louis Lepoutre, T 02 347 3429

Librairie Saint-Hubert
Bertrand Niaudet opened Librairie Saint-Hubert in the middle of the grand, marbled arcade of galerie du Roi in 2006. A bookshop since 1941, the listed interior of this former pharmacy has been opened up to create a mezzanine gallery space lined with a delicate art nouveau steel balustrade. Here, regular exhibitions are held to promote picture-book publications from the likes of pop artist Jim Dine and multimedia artist Jacques Villeglé. Librarie Saint-Hubert covers subjects such as fine art, architecture, sculpture and design, but the widest selection of titles is on photography. Given the store's central location, a number of more touristy publications are also on offer.
2 galerie du Roi, T 02 511 2412,
librairie-saint-hubert.com

Daniel Perahia
This interiors store displays items that reveal architect/owner Daniel Perahia's flair for selecting choice pieces. Classics from Carl Hansen sit alongside newer designs like the pendant 'Torch' lights by rising Belgian star Sylvain Willenz for Established & Sons. A sample of the vast library of reference texts sits on the ply shelving by Moormann, which is stocked exclusively in Brussels. The residential scale of the showroom area, complete with marble mantelpieces, is particularly appropriate for displaying the works on sale here. For a wider range of high-end pieces, drop by Instore (T 02 344 9637) or Flamant (T 02 514 4707).
63 quai au Bois à Brûler, T 02 223 3890, danielperahia.be

Martin Margiela
Bruxellois fashion tastes lean towards the avant garde, and this is the shop to visit to find those coveted Margiela pieces that aren't normally stocked in London or Paris. The white-on-white trompe-l'œil interior of this compact corner boutique is typical Margiela. Anything ugly, including coathangers, is hidden under neat white cloth covers. The various lines of the fashion house are demarcated by different flooring – the evolving men's wardrobe has worn wooden boards and marble tiles signal the women's basics.
114 rue de Flandre, T 02 223 7520, maisonmartinmargiela.com

Pierre Marcolini

The luxuriously appointed two-storey shop of Pierre Marcolini, Brussels' upstart chocolatier, is more haute couture boutique than chocolate larder. Collections are displayed with museum-like precision on Delvaux-designed trays. The chocolate tablets move Ritter Sport on a step or two, but at a price, while the nougat and marshmallows are equally delicious. It's also worth trying the back-to-front atelier of Zaabär (T 02 533 9580), a new arrival on the scene and audacious for its scale alone. Industrial chocolate-making equipment is street-facing while the beautifully presented vacuum-packed goods are to the rear. For a more down-to-earth tea-room atmosphere, head to Frederic Blondeel (T 02 502 2131).
1 rue des Minimes, T 02 514 1206, marcolini.com

Soho
Nestling among the high-end chain stores of avenue Louise and Place Stephanie is the independent outlet Soho. Its own-brand, Italian-made men's and women's lines are both stylish and witty, and are presented within an interior that is just plain fun. The industrial-chic playfulness is seen in the upturned firebuckets used as lampshades and shelving made out of wine barrels, while the electrics are made visible in glass-covered trenches. The exposed brick walls are plastered in a cowhide or cloud pattern depending on your take, and provide a space for up-and-coming artists to exhibit their work.
6 place Stephanie, T 02 503 1469, sohofashion.be

Emery & Cie

Despite first appearances, this is not solely a tile shop. Frustrated by struggling to find what she needed as an architect, Agnès Emery produced a range of paints. Now, as aficionados will tell you, her product range extends to wallpapers, rugs, fabrics, wrought-iron furniture, tableware and lighting. However, there is no question that tiles dominate the ground-floor entrance of her store, which stretches across three houses. Made from cement, they can be customised with a choice of more than 250 patterns and 48 colours. The shop is laid out in a series of room sets, and products might be displayed in a Moorish bathroom or on a four-poster bed. A London showroom opened in 2008 but orders still go through Brussels.
27 rue de l'Hôpital, T 02 513 5892,
www.emeryetcie.com

SPORTS AND SPAS
WORK OUT, CHILL OUT OR JUST WATCH

Exercise does not feature highly on the agenda of the *Bruxellois*. Even the influence of national hero and five-times Tour de France winner Eddy Merckx has not persuaded many locals to take to two wheels. In addition to the hilly topography and poor cycle paths, there's a general free-for-all on the roads, all of which has thwarted the success of the rental scheme Cyclocity (www.cyclocity.be). This is a real shame, as the city is ideally seen by bike.

For runners, the central Parc de Bruxelles is more suited to the casual jogger than the serious runner. To get some kilometres under your belt, try the Bois de la Cambre to the south-east, a real forest with countless paths. For those who prefer to keep fit indoors, top-flight gyms are scarce, the best being the members-only David Lloyd (41 drève de Lorraine, T 02 534 9000) beside the Bois de la Cambre. Swimmers are a little better catered for. Good venues include the art deco Victor Boin (38 rue de la Perche, T 02 539 0615) and Bains de la Ville de Bruxelles (28 rue du Chevreuil, T 02 511 2468), where the pool is on the top floor.

Many of the city's best spas are located in hotels or gyms. This lack of specialisation unfortunately diminishes any sense of escape or exclusivity. An exception is the Serendip Spa (see p092). The numerous salons and nail bars in town will help you keep up with the more superficial aspects of your beauty regime.

For full addresses, see Resources.

Stone Age

Hidden within the Woluwe-Saint-Lambert sports facility is the Stone Age climbing centre. Inside this Tardis-like space, a kaleidoscopic array of screw-in holds mark out some 95 climbs, catering for various levels of expertise. Each route can be pre-analysed on the centre's website. The longest climb is 22m, and considering the ceiling height is only 15m, this gives an indication of the degree of overhang.

Should trips up L'Arch, Le Prism, Le Grand Dévers, Le Bloc or the concrete-and-brick external wall not challenge you enough, a dangle from La Goutte (Drop) ought to be a test. The ropes are already fixed and all the equipment can be rented.
Center Sportif de la Woluwe, 87 avenue Mounier, T 02 777 1305, stone-age.be

King Baudouin Stadium
Rebuilt and renamed in 2000 following the 1985 Heysel disaster, the original entrance façade of this stadium, designed by Joseph Van Neck in 1930, nudges out from a harsh plane of red brick. There is now an athletics track around the football pitch, and the tragedy is commemorated by a 60 sq m stainless-steel sundial with a light for each of the 39 victims.
155/2 avenue du Marathon, T 02 474 3940

Serendip Spa

Half-Sri Lankan, half-English founder Claudia Zackariya-Dau established Serendip when she couldn't find a day spa that met her needs in Brussels. The darkwood flooring, deep-pink and burnt-orange interiors, and Balinese throws on the beds in the six treatment rooms are a deliberate step away from the svelte, white Scandinavian slant found in many of the city's other spas. Organic products from Li'tya, an Australian range, are used in a wide spectrum of treatments that include Balinese, Ayurvedic and Tibetan massage, which combines Thai-style pressure and long Swedish movements. As with most of the treatments, it is delivered by a therapist from the country of origin.
18 place Stephanie, T 02 503 5504, www.serendipspa.com

Nemo 33
The world's deepest dive pool sinks to a full 35m (about 12 storeys), despite its name. Designed by engineer and owner John Beernaerts with architect Sebastian Moreno Vacca, the white-tiled interior is split into various levels and water is kept at a balmy 30 degrees, partially heated by rooftop solar panels.
333 rue de Stalle, T 02 332 3334, nemo33.com

ESCAPES

WHERE TO GO IF YOU WANT TO LEAVE TOWN

Getting away from Brussels can begin with a painful stop-start journey along the ring road; a rush hour or two that begins fairly early on a Friday afternoon. Consider taking the train east to the Calatrava-designed Gare Liège-Guillemins (see p102). This is the gateway to the hills of the Ardennes, where you'll find many good spas and the F1 racetrack at Spa-Francorchamps. The route northwest from the city crosses the plains of Flanders taking you to the Channel coast and Knokke-Heist – the resort of choice for Brussels' beautiful people. If you're driving, your language skills will be tested, as signs switch between French and Flemish seemingly at random. Anvers for Antwerp and Mons for Bergen are understandable; trickier are Jodoigne for Geldenaken and Tirlemont for Tienen.

Aside from the bucolic delights of the Ardennes, there are plenty of other easy escapes from Brussels. Antwerp is a great shopping destination, while Ghent and Bruges deliver picturesque medieval architecture. Tracing the military battles fought on Belgian soil is a sobering experience, particularly with the daily sounding of the *Last Post* at the Menin Gate outside Ypres. Easier to access are the battlefields of Waterloo, where the steep slopes of the Butte du Lion memorial take centre stage. Equally, the Royal Museum for Central Africa at Tervuren (see p100) and the inclined lock system at Ronquières on the Charleroi-Brussels canal should not be missed. *For full addresses, see Resources.*

Carbon Hotel, Genk
Despite being dotted with disused colliery gear and slag heaps, the landscape surrounding Genk is surprisingly cheerful. But make no mistake, the reason to visit this city, located 95km east of the capital, is the Carbon Hotel. Its striking restaurant, Carbon Taste (above), offers an extensive menu based on the local *terroir*; the Enomatic wine-by-the-glass system at the adjacent bar includes Limburg wines among others. The top-floor Carbon Sense spa (overleaf) is the yang to the hotel's yin. Its white interiors include a *badhuis* (bath house), with two saunas and a hammam with a heated treatment slab. The 60 guest rooms are indulgently large and feature open bathrooms zoned by raised stone or metallic mosaic floors.
38 Europalaan, T 08 932 2920, carbonhotel.be

Carbon Sense spa, Carbon Hotel, Genk

RMCA, Tervuren
Just on the edge of the tram network to the east of Brussels is the village of Tervuren, notable for its beautiful lakes and parkland. It's also home to the Royal Museum for Central Africa (RMCA), built in 1897 to showcase King Leopold II's Congo Free State. The most impressive approach is via the gardens (above). Look out for the use of the king's initials as a decorative element in the window mantels and the stucco ceiling of the entrance rotunda. The museum dwells with scathing brevity on the tragedy of Belgium's colonial past, but does include many African exhibits.
13 Leuvensesteenweg, T 02 769 5211, www.africamuseum.be

Gare Liège-Guillemins, Liège
A mere 40 minutes from Brussels by high-speed train is the soaring glass-and-steel canopy of Liège-Guillemins station. Completed in 2008, its ribbed arcs float high above the platforms, while pedestrian walkways beneath the tracks attempt to reunite two sides of the city. If the sweeping majesty of Santiago Calatrava's station is not enough of a draw, then the Ron Arad-designed steel lattice roof that snakes through Liège's Médiacité shopping centre should be worth the price of your train ticket when it opens in late 2009. Refuel with some excellent Belgian fare at Table à Thé (T 04 232 2052), a fine-dining experience worthy of the capital.
2 place des Guillemins

NOTES
SKETCHES AND MEMOS

RESOURCES
CITY GUIDE DIRECTORY

A
Alexis Vanhove 024
 61 rue Émile Bouilliot
Alice 072
 182 rue Antoine Dansaert
 T 02 513 3307
 alicebxl.com
Almine Rech Gallery 026
 14 rue de Praetere
 T 02 648 5684
 galeriealminerech.com
L'Archiduc 038
 6 rue Antoine Dansaert
 T 02 512 0652
 archiduc.net
L'Artea 037
 940 chaussée de Waterloo
 T 02 372 0979
Atomium 058
 Square de l'Atomium
 Boulevard du Centenaire
 T 02 475 4747
 atomium.be
Au Vieux Saint Martin 036
 38 place du Grand Sablon
 T 02 512 6476
 nielsbrothers.com

B
Bains de la Ville de Bruxelles 088
 28 rue du Chevreuil
 T 02 511 2468
Le Balmoral 046
 21 place Georges Brugmann
 T 02 347 0882
 sites.resto.com/balmoral
Bar du Matin 044
 172 chaussée d'Alsemberg
 T 02 537 7159

Basilique du Sacré-Cœur de Koekelberg 009
 1 parvis de la Basilique
 T 02 425 8822
Bazaar 051
 63 rue de Capucins
 T 02 511 2600
 bazaarresto.be
Belga Queen 032
 32 rue du Fossé aux Loups
 T 02 217 2187
 belgaqueen.be
Belgacom Towers 014
 Koning Albert II-laan
Berlaymont 010
 200 rue de la Loi
Bij den Boer 032
 60 quai aux Briques
 T 02 512 6122
 bijdenboer.com
Bonsoir Clara 048
 22-26 rue Antoine Dansaert
 T 02 502 0990
 bonsoirclara.be
La Boussole 032
 61 quai du Bois à Brûler
 T 02 218 5877
 laboussole-be.com
Brasseries Georges 042
 259 avenue Winston Churchill
 T 02 347 2100
 brasseriesgeorges.be
Les Brigittines 060
 1 petite rue des Brigittines
 T 02 213 8610
 www.brigittines.be

C

Café des Spores 045
103-108 chaussée d'Alsemberg
T 02 534 1303
cafedesspores.be

Café Walvis 034
209 rue Antoine Dansaert
T 02 219 9532
cafewalvis.be

La Canne en Ville 033
22 rue de la Réforme
T 02 347 2926
www.lacanneenville.be

La Cantine de la Ville 054
72 rue Haute
T 02 512 8898
cantinedelaville.be

CBR Administrative Offices 057
185 chaussée de la Hulpe

Central Station 067
2 carrefour de l'Europe

Chez Moeder Lambic 039
68 rue de Savoie
T 02 544 1699

Chez Richard 036
2 rue des Minimes
T 02 512 1406

Christophe Coppens 072
23 place du Nouveau Marché aux Grains
T 02 538 0813
christophecoppens.com

Comme Chez Soi 031
23 place Rouppe
T 02 512 2921
www.commechezsoi.be

Cospaia 052
1 rue Capitaine Crespel
T 02 513 0303
cospaia.be

Cyclocity 088
T 09 001 1000
www.cyclocity.be

D

Daniel Perahia 080
63 quai au Bois à Brûler
T 02 223 3890
danielperahia.be

David Lloyd 088
41 drève de Lorraine
T 02 534 9000
davidlloyd.be

E

Emery & Cie 085
27 rue de l'Hôpital
T 02 513 5892
www.emeryetcie.com

En Face de Parachute 032
578 chaussée de Waterloo
T 02 346 4741

F

Faisons un Rêve 077
112 avenue Louis Lepoutre
T 02 347 3429

Fin de Siècle 047
9 rue des Chartreux

Flagey 013
Place Sainte-Croix
T 02 641 1020
www.flagey.be

Flamant 080
36 place du Grand Sablon
T 02 514 4707
flamant.com

Fontainas 047
91 rue Marché au Charbon
T 02 503 3112

Frederic Blondeel 082
24 quai aux Briques
T 02 502 2131
frederic-blondeel.be

Fuse 051
*208 rue Blaes
T 02 511 9789
fuse.be*

G
Gare Liège-Guillemins 102
*2 place des Guillemins
Liège*
Gaudron 025
*3 place Georges Brugmann
T 02 343 9790
gaudron.be*
Generali Real Estate Investments 057
187-189 chaussée de la Hulpe
Gladstone Gallery 026
*12 rue du Grand Cerf
T 02 513 3531
gladstonegallery.com*
Glaverbel 070
166 chaussée de la Hulpe

H
Horta Museum 067
*25 rue Américaine
T 02 543 0490
www.hortamuseum.be*
Hôtel Hannon 062
*1 avenue de la Jonction
T 02 538 4220
contretype.org*

I
Idiz Bogam 076
*76 rue Antoine Dansaert
T 02 512 1032*
Instore 080
*90 rue Tenbosch
T 02 344 9637
instore.be*

L'Intemporelle 046
*114 avenue Louis Lepoutre
T 02 345 9893*

J
Jack O'Shea's 033
*30 rue le Titien
T 02 732 5351
jackoshea.com*
Jacques Brol 072
*202 rue Haute
T 0476 250 253*

K
Kaat Tilley 072
*6 galerie du Roi
T 02 510 0012
kaattilley.com*
Kamo 054
*123 avenue des Saisons
T 02 648 7848*
Kif Kif Café 030
*1 square Biarritz
T 02 644 1810*
King Baudouin Stadium 090
*155/2 avenue du Marathon
T 02 474 3940*
Knokke Out 054
*7 Astridlaan
Knokke-Heist
T 05 060 1226*

L
Librairie Saint-Hubert 078
*2 galerie du Roi
T 02 511 2412
librairie-saint-hubert.com*

Lola 036
33 place du Grand Sablon
T 02 514 2460
restolola.be

M
Mademoiselle Jean 076
100 rue Antoine Dansaert
T 02 513 5069
www.mademoisellejean.com
Mamma Roma 032
5 rue du Page
T 02 544 1402
La Manufacture 050
12-20 rue Notre-Dame du Sommeil
T 02 502 2525
manufacture.be
Martin Margiela 081
114 rue de Flandre
T 02 223 7520
maisonmartinmargiela.com
Menin Gate 096
Ypres
www.lastpost.be
Michel Lambrecht 020
18 rue Watteeu
T 02 502 2729
Mirano Continental 051
38 chaussée de Louvain
T 02 227 3942
mirano.be
Modes 054
164 rue Blaes
T 02 512 4907
Museum & Gardens Van Buuren 028
41 avenue Leo Errera
T 02 343 4851
museumvanbuuren.com

N
Natan 073
158 avenue Louise
T 02 647 1001
www.natan.be
Natan XIII 073
101 rue Antoine Dansaert
T 02 514 1517
Nemo 33 094
333 rue de Stalle
T 02 332 3334
nemo33.com
Noctis 032
noctis.com

P
Palais de Justice 012
Place Poelaert
T 02 508 6410
Pierre Marcolini 082
1 rue des Minimes
T 02 514 1206
marcolini.com
Porte de Hal 009
boulevard du Midi
T 02 534 1518
www.mrah.be
Portrait de Famille 032
165a rue Franz Merjay
T 02 344 3712
www2.resto.be/portraitdefamille
Privé Joke 054
76-78 rue Marché au Charbon
T 02 502 6367
privejoke.be

Q
La Quincaillerie 032
 45 rue du Page
 T 02 533 9833
 quincaillerie.be

R
Recyclart 051
 25 rue des Ursulines
 T 02 289 0059
 recyclart.be
Restaurant Vincent 042
 8-10 rue des Dominicains
 T 02 511 2607
 restaurantvincent.com
Riverwoods Channel Club 054
 832b Zeedjik-Het Zoute
 Knokke-Heist
 T 05 062 8404
Roue d'Or 042
 26 rue des Chapeliers
 T 02 514 2554
Royal Museum for Central Africa 100
 13 Leuvensesteenweg
 Tervuren
 T 02 769 5211
 www.africamuseum.be

S
St Augustin Church 064
 Place de l'Altitude Cent
 T 02 344 5956
Salle de Machines 068
 364 avenue Van Volxem
 T 02 343 2004
 blib.be
Scènes de Ménage 024
 4 place Georges Brugmann
 T 02 344 3295

Sea Grill 032
 Radisson SAS Royal Hotel
 47 rue de Fossé aux Loups
 T 02 227 9225
 seagrill.be
Serendip Spa 092
 18 place Stephanie
 T 02 503 5504
 www.serendipspa.com
Soho 084
 6 place Stephanie
 T 02 503 1469
 sohofashion.be
Stef's Antique Hall 072
 63 rue Blaes
 stefantiek.com
Stijl 076
 74 rue Antoine Dansaert
 T 02 512 0313
Stone Age 089
 Center Sportif de la Woluwe
 87 avenue Mounier
 T 02 777 1305
 stone-age.be

T
Table à Thé 102
 15 rue des Carmes
 Liège
 T 04 232 2052
 www.tableathe.be
Taverne Greenwich 047
 7 rue des Chartreux
 T 02 511 4167
Le Tavernier 054
 445 chaussée de Boondael
 T 02 640 7191

Taxis & Tours complex 056
Royal Warehouse
86c avenue du Port
T 02 420 6069
tourtaxis.com
La Terrasse de l'Hippodrome 054
51-53 chaussée de la Hulpe
T 02 354 7200
www.la-terrasse.be
Le Typographe 072
167 rue Franz Merjay
T 02 345 1676

U
Underwear 072
47 rue Antoine Dansaert
T 02 514 2731
dunderwear.be

V
Victor Boin 088
38 rue de la Perche
T 02 539 0615
VUB Rectorate 066
2 boulevard de la Plaine

W
Waffles 074
189 rue Antoine Dansaert
T 02 219 0575
ilovewaffles.be
Wiels 068
354 avenue Van Volxem
T 02 340 0050
wiels.org
Winery 046
18 place Georges Brugmann
T 02 345 4717
wineryonline.be

X
Xavier Hufkens 026
6-8 rue Saint-Georges
T 02 639 6730
xavierhufkens.com

Z
Zaabär 082
125 chaussée de Charleroi
T 02 533 9580
zaabar.be

HOTELS
ADDRESSES AND ROOM RATES

Aloft Brussels Schuman 016
Room rates:
prices on request
Place Jean Rey
T 02 224 3199
starwoodhotels.com/alofthotels

Hotel Amigo 020
Room rates:
double, €600;
Presidential Suite René Magritte, €3,500
1-3 rue de l'Amigo
T 02 547 4747
hotelamigo.com

Be Manos 022
Room rates:
double, from €140;
Junior Suite, from €210
23 square de l'Aviation
T 02 520 6565
bemanos.com

Hotel Bloom 018
Room rates:
double, from €90;
Rooms 209, 331 and 326, from €90
250 rue Royale
T 02 220 6611
www.hotelbloom.com

Hotel Café Pacific 017
Room rates:
double, from €150;
Mezzanine Room 201, from €190
57 rue Antoine Dansaert
T 02 213 0080
hotelcafepacific.com

Carbon Hotel 097
Room rates:
double, €250
38 Europalaan
Genk
T 08 932 2920
carbonhotel.be

Chambres en Ville 016
Room rates:
double, from €90
19 rue de Londres
T 02 512 9290
www.chambresenville.be

Crowne Plaza Brussels
City Centre – Le Palace 016
Room rates:
double, €400
3 rue Gineste
T 02 203 6200
ichotelsgroup.com

The Dominican 023
Room rates:
double, €425;
Twin Deluxe Room 531, €475;
Junior Suite €750
9 rue Leopold
T 02 203 0808
thedominican.be

Hooy Kaye Lodge 016
Room rates:
double, from €95
22 quai aux Pierres de Taille
T 02 218 4440
hooykayelodge.com

Hotel Metropole 016
Room rates:
double, €390
31 place de Brouckère
T 02 217 2300
www.metropolehotel.com

Royal Windsor Hotel 016
Room rates:
double, from €140;
Fashion Room, from €575
5 rue Duquesnoy
T 02 505 5555
warwickhotels.com

Sofitel Brussels Le Louise 016
Room rates:
double, from €110
40 avenue de la Toison d'Or
T 02 514 2200
sofitel.com

The White Hotel 021
Room rates:
double, from €80;
Super White, from €100
212 avenue Louise
T 02 644 2929
thewhitehotel.be

WALLPAPER* CITY GUIDES

Editorial Director
Richard Cook

Art Director
Loran Stosskopf

Editor
Rachael Moloney

Author
Guy Dittrich

Deputy Editor
Jeremy Case

Managing Editor
Jessica Diamond

Chief Designer
Daniel Shrimpton

Designer
Lara Collins

Map Illustrator
Russell Bell

Photography Editor
Sophie Corben

Photography Assistant
Robin Key

Sub-Editor
Rachel Ward

Editorial Assistant
Ella Marshall

Interns
Kim Fischer
Cat Tsang
Yvette Yarnold

Wallpaper* Group
Editor-in-Chief
Tony Chambers

Publishing Director
Gord Ray

Contributors
Uli Birner
Chris Bourne
Phoebe Burnett
Marion Flipse
Benoit Hellings
Sara Henrichs
Nicholas Lewis
Meirion Pritchard
Andy Round
Ellie Stathaki

Wallpaper* ® is a registered trademark of IPC Media Limited

All prices are correct at time of going to press, but are subject to change.

PHAIDON

Phaidon Press Limited
Regent's Wharf
All Saints Street
London N1 9PA

Phaidon Press Inc
180 Varick Street
New York, NY 10014

Phaidon® is a registered trademark of Phaidon Press Limited

www.phaidon.com

First published 2009
© 2009 IPC Media Limited

ISBN 978 0 7148 4907 2

A CIP Catalogue record for this book is available from the British Library.

All rights reserved.
No part of this publication may be reproduced, stored in a retrieval system or transmitted, in any form or by any means, electronic, mechanical, photocopying, recording or otherwise, without the prior permission of Phaidon Press.

Printed in China

PHOTOGRAPHERS

Sarah Blee
Bar du Matin, p044

Benjamin Blossom
Brussels city view,
inside front cover
Berlaymont, pp010-011
Palais de Justice, p012
Flagey, p013
Belgacom Towers,
pp014-015
Hotel Café Pacific, p017
Hotel Bloom!, pp018-019
Hotel Amigo, p020
The White Hotel, p021
Be Manos, p022
The Dominican, p023
Gaudron, p025
Xavier Hufkens, pp026-027
Museum Van Buuren,
pp028-029
Kif Kif Café, p030
Comme Chez Soi, p031
Le Canne en Ville, p033
Café Walvis, pp034-035
Lola, p036
L'Artea, p037
L'Archiduc, p038
Chez Moeder Lambic,
p039, pp040-041
Brasseries Georges,
pp042-043

Café des Spores, p045
Le Balmoral, p046
Taverne Greenwich, p047
Bonsoir Clara, pp048-049
Le Manufacture, p050
Cospaia, pp052-053
Céline Pécheux, p055
CBR Administrative
Offices, p057
Atomium, pp058-059
Les Brigittines, pp060-061
Hôtel Hannon, p062, p063
St Augustin Church,
pp064-065
Horta Museum, p067
Wiels, pp068-069
Glaverbel, pp070-071
Natan XIII, p073
Waffles, pp074-075
Stijl, p076
Faisons un Rêve, p077
Librarie Saint-Hubert,
pp078-079
Daniel Perahia, p080
Martin Margiela, p081
Pierre Marcolini,
pp082-083
Soho, p084
Emery & Cie, p085,
pp086-087
Stone Age, p089
King Baudouin Stadium,
pp090-091
Serendip Spa, pp092-093
Nemo 33, pp094-095

Bernadette Mergaerts
VUB Rectorate, p066

Roger Mapp/Alamy
RMCA, pp100-101

**Wolfgang Schwager/
Artur**
Gare Liège-Guillemins,
pp102-103

BRUSSELS
A COLOUR-CODED GUIDE TO THE HOT 'HOODS

UPPER TOWN
The wide boulevards and park squares are lined with imposing palaces and museums

ST JOSSE AND SCHAERBEEK
Sleek glass skyscrapers are clustered around the functionalist block of Gare du Nord

ST GILLES AND FOREST
Come here for impressive views over Brussels and some superb art nouveau architecture

EU QUARTER AND ETTERBEEK
This area is dominated by landmark EU buildings, and watering holes for the bureaucrats

LOWER TOWN
The maze of streets leading off Grand Place is home to the city's best fashion boutiques

JETTE, LAEKEN AND HEYSEL
A canalside redevelopment is giving this nondescript residential district a lease of life

IXELLES AND UCCLE
This well-to-do part of town is popular with expats and has a lively bar and gastro scene

ANDERLECHT AND MOLENBEEK
The city's former industrial centre is beginning to show the first signs of gentrification

For a full description of each neighbourhood, see the Introduction.
Featured venues are colour-coded, according to the district in which they are located.